What's your teaching identity?

Helen Waldron

What's your Teacher Identity?
by Helen Waldron

Academic Study Kit
81 Northwood Avenue
Brighton BN2 8RG
East Sussex
ENGLAND

www.academicstudykit.com

First published 2016

Editor: Catriona Watson-Brown

Design and layout: Ziaul Haque

ISBN 978-0-9956701-1-2

Printed in England

Acknowledgements

Thanks go to my parents, John and Margaret Waldron, who gave me and all of their children a sense of continuity, a sense of our own individuality and the courage to express ourselves.

Likewise my husband Richard and my sons, Connor and Laurence, because families (apart from everything else!) set our priorities and help us progress meaningfully.

The members of my local teaching organisation HELTA, who provided a sounding board for some of the ideas in this book.

I would like to thank Ziaul Haque for the cover and and in-book design and my editor Catriona Watson-Brown, whose perception and sensibility make her a joy to work with.

Great kudos goes to my publisher, Julie Pratten, who has the courage to follow her instinct and produce content that is simply different. I'm proud to be the first writer in what will no doubt prove to be a thought-provoking and ground-breaking series of works.

Introduction

Identity, in its many forms, is a very complex issue. Working in ELT, we are confronted with notions of cultural[1] and linguistic[2] identities on an almost daily basis; the mixed-national language classroom can bring its own issues of ethnic and national identies; an understanding of others' religious identities frequently leads us to modify our lesson content.

We are encouraged to reflect on such issues after every lesson we teach. Indeed, reflecting, defining and giving feedback are very often what we do best. Yet how often do we reflect on our own identities as teachers, especially given the myriad of situations we can find ourselves teaching in? Moving from culture to culture is hugely enriching and often a prime motivation behind this choice of career. We develop a genuine interest in our students' development, yet at the same time we need to be aware of our value and our limits within any learning situation. Awareness leads to the courage to be

1

yourself, and this in turn is what drives change, in identity as in all other fields.

Just think how the concept of gender identity has evolved. From the 'working man' and 'little woman' of a century ago, to the growing acceptance of same-sex relationships, to questioning the whole concept of there being fixed genders. Similarly, the greatest achievement of the last few Paralympic Games has been the shift of perception from how admirable these disabled people are to attempt sports to what admirable sportspeople they are. Seeing Paralympians fighting for the right to compete in the regular Olympic games is a demonstration of the shift in disability identity. So how does all this relate to teaching?

Work

"I'm trying to do it my way. For me to be happy in the business means I have to do it myself."

Julian Cope, musician

When I asked some experienced teachers at my local teaching association to describe their teaching identity in one word or expression, they came up with such answers as 'spirit', 'dedicated', 'passionate', 'creative' and 'innovative'. Admittedly, it's very hard to define your working life in just one word or expression, but I was struck by the introspective nature of all of these self-observations. Nobody said 'professional' or 'experienced' or 'struggling' or whatever. All their responses show the teacher in the classroom or preparing the lesson and looking inwards. (As I have already mentioned, as a profession we do reflection well!)

When I researched a suitable definition of identity, I came across the following three recurring elements:

- What sets you apart and makes you recognisable
- What remains unchanged when circumstances change
- The quality or condition of being exactly the same as something else (what you belong to)

What sets you apart and makes you recognisable.

This might be certain skills or preferences, or personal characteristics and opinions, which others don't share. You might be aware of this and consider it your USP (unique selling point) or even see it as a component of your 'brand'. This is how others see you and also how you choose to present yourself. In the context of your teaching identity, you may be the young learners expert, the experienced teacher trainer, the go-to person in the field of research into examination methodology, or simply the extremely patient / understanding / conscientious teacher.

What remains unchanged when circumstances change

This is your essence, your core. It's how people instinctively perceive you, and also your ingrained reactions and perceptions. These can weaken or strengthen over time, but are generally very deep-seated qualities. In the context of your teaching identity, your core may be your default mode of patience, understanding, conscientiousness. It may also be your deep-rooted beliefs about teaching and learning and methodologies. Additionally, it could be related to your perception of others and, as a result, affect your interpersonal relationships with your students, colleagues and clients.

The quality or condition of being exactly the same as something else[3]

This is what you belong to. It is you as a reflection of your environment. It acknowledges your adherence to a movement, belief, profession, ideal or organisation. In the context of your teaching identity, it includes the type of institution you work for, or whether you work entirely on your own. It also includes whether you choose to join a large established ELT organisation like TESOL or IATEFL, or whether you prefer more dedicated grassroots groups like TaWSIG. Perhaps you belong to all of these organisations and others besides. They do not have to be ELT organisations to be work-related. You can join Toastmasters to garner custom for your presentation seminar, and become a member of your local Chamber of Commerce to network with other potential clients. You may argue that you're a member of these groups for purely professional reasons, but the fact is, all these groups say something about you to others – and to yourself. The degree to which you're active in these organisations, of course, also says something about you. You will see yourself mirrored in the other participants, and if you really don't like what you see, you will soon find reasons not to attend events or get involved. At best, you will remain as a passive member.

It's interesting that my sample of answers from the teaching association all fit into the first or the second of these categories (or both, of course – to decide which would involve deeper analysis). None of them came close to belonging in the third.

All onus and no bonus?

"Happiness can exist only in acceptance."

George Orwell

So are my teaching association colleagues too inward looking? Perhaps it's a result of their own high standards, spurred on by the millions of inspirational lists, which often masquerade under the category of 'professional development' (as the one below[4] does). You may not agree with them, but they are hard to ignore. This is a randomly sourced example entitled '11 habits of an effective teacher'. Apparently, an effective teacher (in capital letters, so teachers are being shouted at!):

1	ENJOYS TEACHING
2	MAKES A DIFFERENCE
3	SPREADS POSITIVITY
4	GETS PERSONAL
5	GIVES 100%
6	STAYS ORGANISED
7	IS OPEN-MINDED
8	HAS STANDARDS
9	FINDS INSPIRATION
10	EMBRACES CHANGE
11	CREATES REFLECTIONS.

Each of these eleven points is valid, yet it's still only half of the story. There's no suggestion of outside support or of context, both of which are also vital for a teacher to be effective.

The trouble is, this largely one-sided status quo means that a teacher could be classed as amazingly effective according to the eleven criteria above, but still be unable to remain in the profession due to lack of support. What's more, the carrots are being dangled by the carrot salesmen themselves. Recognised ELT qualifications such as CELTA, DELTA and Trinity Cert Tesol quite rightly set high standards for classroom practice. However, most people are expected to pay for it privately, take the time off to devote to study and still have no guarantee of steady work with decent pay on successful completion. If you need to make a living from teaching, all this needs to be factored into the decision.

A *Guardian Education* article entitled 'Beyond CELTA'[5] gives a fairly balanced overview of the pros and cons of doing a DELTA, mentioning the expense of the qualification, the time needed to do it and the fact that you may not necessarily be accepted for the course – successful applicants are likely to have experienced learning and development 'in a "good" language school' from 'in-service training and/or staffroom banter'.

The latter may seem to be an odd management training measure, but that's often how it works in ELT. You either get your professional development on the job informally and for free or you pay through the nose.

While this may be a more-or-less understandable fact of life for CELTA, it makes less sense for DELTA. This diploma is for experienced and established teachers within 'good' language schools, yet the majority of teachers taking it still pay for it themselves. Language schools rarely subsidise this aspect of professional development which they then benefit from.

There's an old training adage from the world of permanent employment:

'What happens if we invest in developing people and they leave us?'

'Yes, but what happens if we don't and they stay?'

I think the ELT version would read:

'What happens if we simply make it clear that the onus is on them?'

'Good idea. And if they don't like it, well, there's plenty more where they came from.'

The reasons given in the above-mentioned article for doing a DELTA are:

- career progression
- demonstrating commitment
- deepening understanding of teaching and learning
- improving classroom performance
- confidence
- economics (in many cases a DELTA-qualified teacher will receive – *and really should receive* – a salary increment). [my italics]

Again, the teacher is required to invest in themselves with absolutely no guarantee of any return on investment from the side of the language school or industry. There will be career opportunities, but no automatic progression or recognition of superiority. Wanting to improve your classroom performance and grow in confidence as a teacher is admirable and valid, but (despite what the mythical teacher who gives 100% may claim) it's often the recognition from others, in particular your employers, which rounds off the achievement. I think of my experienced teachers pouring their spirit, passion, creativity and innovation into their working life. And in return they are 'rewarded' by being required to spend their hard-earned money on a product that those who can better afford it will benefit from more.

The best of jobs, the worst of jobs

"Everything about me is a contradiction, and so is everything about everybody else. We are made out of oppositions; we live between two poles. There's a philistine and an aesthete in all of us, and a murderer and a saint. You don't reconcile the poles. You just recognize them."

Orson Welles, actor

I love English language teaching. It's one of the few jobs where the human contact still outweighs the paperwork. I'm lucky enough to have the freedom to structure my courses at my own discretion, which makes it more creative than a lot of teaching is nowadays. I teach in-company, enjoy every minute and leave each company grateful that I don't have to work in the same place five days a week, 45-odd weeks a year. I flatter myself that my students enjoy the lessons as a change from their daily routine, and by all reports I get to see them at their best as a result.

At the same time, I know it's unrequited love. Bad pay, no prospects, an obligation to develop yourself professionally, coupled with the assumption that you will perform the double whammy of sending yourself to conferences and workshops at your own expense, while cancelling your regular work and missing out on a week's income to do so. Not to mention the lack of security, sick pay, pension benefits, paid holiday ... and there's no doubt that secure employment would have enabled me to spend more time with my family, even if that meant accepting unpaid leave. But secure employment and English teaching rarely go hand in hand these days of short-term contract. So, as the old fairground hawker's phrase went, 'You pays your money, you takes your choice.

Confessions of a teacher

Maybe I'm being oversensitive, but am I the only person who holds back when the small talk at a party turns to jobs? I simply find it hard to talk effusively about my work. I don't talk anecdotally about my students for discretionary reasons, neither can I simply give a few self-explanatory facts, whether profession-based ('I'm a doctor') or company-based ('I work for Big Company'). If pushed, I explain that I'm a teacher, but not a teacher that works in a school, not a *real* teacher (yes, I'm sure I have said this), usually before petering out completely.

It's sad and it's because we've failed to take ourselves seriously enough to forge the outward signs of a professional identity by which others can recognise us. Instead of being embarrassed about ourselves, we should be reaping the rewards of all this work and investment we've put in. Actually, I know I'm not alone in this, because when I asked my colleagues a similar question, one of them answered, 'No problem. I simply tell them I'm a journalist.'

I once worked from 8am to 8pm in the week and half days on Saturdays. Sundays were free, so Sundays were when you visited your family or met up with your friends. But we teachers didn't have time to make any. And so we stuck together, spending Sundays shrieking with hollow laughter as one of us looked at our watch and gasped in mock-shock, 'It's nearly time for work!' Because it always was. We went to work several times a day – mornings and afternoons and evenings – with long, useless breaks in between.

This scenario is not unusual, as witnessed by these three anecdotes:

Teacher 1: 'I remember that Friday and Saturday nights were the only nights I really slept properly. I was scared stiff of having to face my "corporate" clients. I was 22 years old with only a three-day Inlingua orientation course under my belt as my TEFL qualification. Helmut Schmidt's daughter was one rising executive at Dresdner Bank I felt intimidated by, and I definitely didn't feel qualified to lead a conversation class with her and her suited peers on global banking issues. So I read *FT Weekend* from cover to cover every Saturday (I remember it was very expensive). And on Sunday nights I woke up in panic every half an hour, fearful of sleeping in. I also remember wandering around Frankfurt on my own on Sundays, sitting in cafés thinking 'How long before I go to work again?' There was the dread, but there was also the relief that I'd actually be able to connect with people who spoke my language again. And wondering if I could afford another pot of coffee to justify sitting in the café any longer.'

Teacher 2: 'When I worked in language schools, we were on contracts so had mornings or long lunchtimes for planning. I never took work home. Since I've started working in universities, though, it's 'plan, teach, plan'. For every ten hours I teach, I need at least another ten to create the lessons, as I always have to create stuff from scratch. I wake up, plan, teach, come home and plan again. If I can stand a late night / early morning, I might manage half a day off on Saturday. This is the life, though, and many other people would happily take on my courses.'

Teacher 3: 'I developed a knack for working on Saturdays, so you only have one day to dread the upcoming week. I taught for eight hours on Saturdays – four two-hour classes with teenagers bouncing off the walls, and my brain bouncing with tiredness – more daycare than teaching. The original meaning of 'pedagogue' springs to mind – it comes from the Greek *paidagogos*, a slave who looked after the master's children. *Plus ça change*.'

More importantly, why do we put up with it? I knew in my case that the students were paying well for lessons and would probably have been horrified to learn how little the teachers were being paid. Sometimes the kinder ones invited my confidence, but I never let on about my personal situation. It was the same reason for my changing the subject at parties – frankly, I was ashamed.

We need to talk

"Knowing what must be done does away with fear."

Rosa Parks, civil rights activist

My personal opinion is that no one should ever be ashamed of their situation. The minute you feel shame, it's time to do something about it. And according to dictionary definitions[6], shame is an emotion intrinsically linked to a sense of consciousness, so you are in a position to acknowledge it and react. So it's actually our fault if we don't deal with it. Right?

Wrong. Shame can come in a shock reaction, but all too often it creeps up on us slowly and insidiously. We live in a culture where the spotlight is on determined authenticity and glittering passion, not on downscaling our expectations and becoming a bit resigned. So we shunt it into the background, sometimes until it's grown so big that we don't know where, when and how to start dealing with it.

Emotions do not evolve in vacuums. There is a great deal of conditioning (culture, society) influencing our perceptions and reactions. According to Wikipedia[7], shame is a 'social emotion' resulting 'from comparison of the self's action with the self's standards'. In the absence of an adequate social element, we are left comparing ourselves with our own standards. And we may be setting them too high to manage on our own. The only solution is for us to take a deep breath and talk to each other. It may feel like we're exposing our innermost fears, but I think we'd be amazed by how many other ELT professionals share those fears.

A strong identity

"It took me quite a long time to develop a voice, and now that I have it, I am not going to be silent."

Madeleine Albright, politician

The link between our inner selves and our outer selves also relies on our awareness of some sort of progression. We need to feel we're moving somewhere, that we're part of a development, even if we don't recognise exactly what it is. The various branches of identity theory are as varied as they are complex, and this is not intended as an academic paper. For the sake of simplicity I would argue that a strong sense of identity centres around the possession of the following three elements:

- a sense of uniqueness
- a sense of affiliation
- a sense of continuity.

Uniqueness

"Be yourself; everyone else is already taken."

Oscar Wilde

A healthy sense of uniqueness is when you have a sense of your own value, you are secure about your unique contribution to your workplace, team, etc., you know you are needed because you can offer something not everyone has. A warning sign is when you can't define exactly what is important about your lessons or your teaching.

Try writing a profile about your teaching self. Imagine you're writing a website text to describe your work and also think about your personal beliefs and reasons for teaching the way you do (a mission statement). After a while, you may be surprised at how much you have to offer!

Affiliation

A healthy sense of affiliation is when you feel you're a part of things. A lot of events can be accessed virtually nowadays, and social media is the modern teacher's classroom (as witnessed by the 'classroom banter' mentioned above). Affiliation can, of course, also refer to you identifying with your work itself. A warning sign is when you feel uncomfortable speaking up within an organisation that claims to be tailored to you and your needs. You might be better taking your subscription fees elsewhere. This also applies to a work situation where you don't identify with the work culture or where you feel underappreciated.

Try to define which aspects disturb you the most. Be as objective as you can, describe them factually and seek feedback from both EFL and non-EFL friends.

Continuity

This is when you recognise your place on some sort of continuum or within a long-term development; you can loosely see how you would have been in some past time and can define yourself within the current situation. Perhaps you can even make plans for the future. This one seems to be somewhat lacking in ELT. The industry is huge, has been going as a business for at least 100 years, and yet I see:

- no models for professional development. As we've seen above, professional development doesn't guarantee you professional advancement. It's demotivating when successful completion of a higher qualification doesn't bring you more benefits than when you started out. Could pay scales and/or recommendations be created for various countries? Could more highly qualified and experienced teachers be rewarded with access to more prestigious projects?
- no role models within the industry (But I'm happy to be proven wrong here; it may well be that many of you have flourished under mentorship from and modelling on someone else, or you may well admire the work of an ELT author.)
- low expectations of support as a result. There's the feeling that all the onus is on the individual teacher to maintain and improve their classroom performance, with little hope of feedback or recognition.

Is there a sense of continuity in the ELT industry or is it really every person for themselves?

Polarities

"Combine the extremes, and you will have the true center."

Karl Wilhelm Friedrich Schlegel, poet

Our lives are full of conflicts. Conflicts are not always negative, but they are issues which need to be resolved in a manner that's authentic for us, in order to move forward. The following technique probably has a very clever name in academic circles, but let's just call it 'the polarities game'. The idea is to jot down the opposite poles of an issue that's preoccupying you, decide how well you are dealing with it, how it impacts on you and what, if anything, you can do about it. You have to think of at least one suggestion. Obviously the conflict will differ from person to person and from situation to situation.

Here's an example for you:

Issue

How much is teaching a 'performing job' and how much can you 'be yourself' in the lesson?

Method

1 Decide whether this is an issue that has preoccupied you in any way. Do you have an instinctive answer to this?

19

2   How well does your instinctive answer correspond to your actual practice?
3   Are there reasons for any divergence?
4   Is there anything you would like to / can change?

My own professional conflicts involve:

- reconciling the cultures of education and business (I'm involved with both simultaneously and they're very different).
- attaining the course aims while teaching adult students without the pressure of exams, etc.
- the need to take time out for professional development vs the need to make money.

Think of three conflicts in your own professional life and define how well you're coming to terms with them. (Warning: once you've defined them, it's no longer possible to completely ignore them!)

If your dilemma isn't symmetrical enough to make a polarity like the issue outlined above, then ask yourself some questions to try and elicit some ideas (be your own teacher!).

Boundaries

"We need to re-create boundaries. When you carry a digital gadget that creates a virtual link to the office, you need to create a virtual boundary that didn't exist before."

Daniel Goleman, writer

People tend not to see ELT teachers as having professional boundaries. Have you ever been in a situation abroad where someone recognised your accent and immediately wanted to practise their English? I hate to say it, but I have two issues with that:

1   We're apparently expected to be teachers 24/7 (which is all the more ironic as we tend to neglect our sense of self). No one would expect a doctor to give them a quick examination at a party. Doctors take themselves more seriously than we do, and it works.

2   People do this without even knowing you're a teacher by profession. The implication is that any native speaker can teach English (and presumably also that no non-native speaker can). I feel belittled.

Like many language trainers who work with one-to-one students and small groups, I embarked at some point on extensive coaching training. If I'm honest, I did this mainly because I often felt I was already coaching my students (sometimes on a very personal level) and I wanted to see how I was meant to be doing it.

Issues such as ethics and boundaries arise very early on in a coaching or counselling training. Ethics – no problem. But boundaries? Can boundaries exist in a world where we're expected to give 100%? Do you know where the boundaries of your work are, and are you able to say no politely when asked to go beyond them? It's OK to say no occasionally. I say this in the knowledge that most readers of this book are more likely to say yes.

Conclusion

There is a wonderful German word *Lebenskünstler*
(literally 'artist of life'), which denotes a person who
approaches life with the zest, inspiration and carefree
attitude of an artist, but at the same time avoids having
to do any 'real' work. My corporate students, who seem
to assume that I live the life of Riley while they have
their noses to the grindstone, frequently try to apply it
to me. I defer, of course, and tell them that with one
thing and another, I work a seven-day week. However,
let's not lose sight of the good things in our search for
recognition, standardisation and a decent wage. We are
creative. Should you decide that, despite the long
history of ELT, there have as yet been no role models
and no models of professional development for us to
base our careers on, then in our search for an identity,
we may have to experiment. Don't be afraid to
experiment. Think David Bowie[8]. Think Cindy
Sherman[9]. Be aware that studies[10] have shown that cases
of schizophrenia are alarmingly high amongst refugees,
who are people living lives wrenched out of context.

Live today, for tomorrow it will all be history. (proverb)

About the author

Helen Waldron started her teaching career in her late teens when she joined the Liverpool adult literacy programme. After three decades running her own in-company language training business in the Hamburg area, she now also coaches and writes. Helen holds an M.Ed. in Applied Linguistics and is a committee member of HELTA. Recently she has contributed to the Heart ELT project A-Z of Hope and co-authored A-Z of Global Issues (Academic Study Kit.)

Notes

1. Transnational Cultural Identity Development is a field of psychology that examines the impact of living and studying abroad on our sense of identity (and on that of our students).

    http://www.sciencedirect.com/science/article/pii/S0962629805000508

    http://isites.harvard.edu/fs/docs/icb.topic1063339.files/rethinkingcultur e.pdf

    http://www.myschedule.jp/icp2016/search/detail_program/id:6476

2. The Sapir-Whorf Hypothesis still forms the basis for studies of how we act and think differently while using different languages.

    http://www.linguisticsociety.org/content/does-language-i-speak-influence-way-i-think

    https://www.cambridge.org/core/journals/bilingualism-language-and-cognition/article/l2-effects-on-l1-event-conceptualization/A63612732FA91CDD231C1092B811ED0D

    http://pss.sagepub.com/content/26/4/518

    http://theconversation.com/how-the-language-you-speak-changes-your-view-of-the-world-40721

3. Henri Tajfel's social identity theory, developed in the late 1970s, takes this idea much further. http://www.simplypsychology.org/social-identity-theory.html

4. http://www.edutopia.org/discussion/11-habits-effective-teacher?utm_source=facebook&utm_medium=socialflow

5. https://www.theguardian.com/education/2008/may/09/tefl. wordsandlanguage

6. www.merriam-webster.com: **shame**: a feeling of guilt, regret, or sadness that you have because *you know* you have done something wrong [my italics] www.thefree**dictionary: shame**: a painful emotion caused by the *awareness* of having done something wrong or foolish [again, my italics]

7. https://en.wikipedia.org/wiki/Shame

8. David Bowie was a British rock star who grew up with family members suffering from mental illness. He was famous for experimenting with his own identity in his early career, to the extent that a psychology book on the subject referenced his name in its title.

   https://www.theguardian.com/science/2016/jun/21/ziggy-stardust-persona-therapy-david-bowie-oliver-james-mental-health?CMP=share_btn_fb

9. Cindy Sherman is an American artist who uses herself as her own canvas and portrays herself in myriad roles in an attempt to explore her own and her collective identity. She was a late child who grew up feeling superfluous in her already complete family.

   https://www.freitag.de/autoren/the-guardian/die-selfie-queen

   https://www.theguardian.com/artanddesign/2016/jul/03/cindy-sherman-interview-retrospective-motivation

10. http://www.bmj.com/content/352/bmj.i1030

www.ingramcontent.com/pod-product-compliance
Lightning Source LLC
Chambersburg PA
CBHW071942020426
42331CB00010B/2980